Praise for
What We Take With Us

Sylvia Woods "captures" the reader in a vault of rich images, layers and layers of ideas to mine, and gorgeously crafted moments of recognition for the poet and for us, her readers. This may be a debut collection, but Woods is no novice to poetry. Each poem is a gem crafted by an experienced hand, strung together jewel after jewel.

— DARNELL ARNOULT
author of *What Travels With Us* and *Galaxie Wagon*

Like switchback roads in the mountains she hails from, Woods' poems zigzag between her work (teaching, writing, keeping house, raising children) and her parents' work (mining, keeping house, raising children). There are hints at family stories and war stories, too. Evident everywhere is her love of music—whether in the literature she's having high school students memorize "to seal . . . in their souls . . . for times of capture" or in dancing with her daddy to A-4 on the jukebox at the café on 421. Woods' poems are going to take you places, and you don't want to miss the ride!

— GEORGE ELLA LYON
Kentucky Poet Laureate 2015-2016; author of *Back to the Light*

The poems in this fine collection are as true as a river fork and as durable as the hills above. They are also, like the many people and voices here recalled, humble and hard-won. The grit and humor walk side by side with grief and spunk, but isn't that what we ask of poetry, this lofty air? As it sails in the breeze of reflection and intellect, don't we also require this ancient art to be human, to be fallible and clumsy and loving and real? This book fulfills those obligations and more. It also walks the poignant line of Time, both knowing and absorbing the fact that one age has unavoidably succeeded another— and yet these poems have hold of both, as if they are kin, and, of course, they are.

— MAURICE MANNING
author of *Railsplitter* and *The Common Man*

What We Take With Us follows a life filled with sweetness and hardship, love and loss, across a lifetime from childhood through parenthood into grandparenthood, as "tangled memory rises, / blackberry and honeysuckle twined." Woven throughout these poems are also the observations and striking moments of a teaching career, where the teacher later realizes that beyond the subject matter, there were also "ghost lessons you didn't know you taught." Woods' poems are grounded in the physical world, where a trip to a café with a father comes to life with music and the smells of "chili, onions frying, / bootleg bourbon and Juicy Fruit, / Old Spice and Irish Spring," where a young boy in a classroom who loves words "twirled the toe of his brogans / on the oiled floor when he forgot a line, / chin pointed to the ceiling." Like the grandmother described in "Crumbs," Woods wastes nothing in this fine collection, sharing with us her people and memories that we will take with us for the long haul.

— JANE SASSER
author of *What's Underneath* and *Itinerant*

Sylvia Woods' *What We Take With Us* is a romp through the joys and pitfalls of teaching, mothering, growing up among siblings and hardworking parents in a small mining community, and coping with the twists and turns of a fully lived life. Characters in Woods' poems are painted in sure, deft strokes—a childhood friend whose head was "a ball of twine with ears," a woman stringing beans with "age detailed hands." From a recollection of "tales that wound // round and round the family tree" like the spiral peelings from a potato to a metaphor of worries stored like wealth in the attic, basement, pantry, cooling in the fridge and ending with a call to "drink life fast, like cheap wine," Woods' poems offer a distinct voice, a slant on life that, after the final poem is read, will send readers back to page one to savor again the deliciousness.

— CONNIE JORDAN GREEN
author of *Household Inventory* and *Darwin's Breath*

Sylvia Woods left a one-room school in the hills, wearing her "grammar girdle," head full of verse to count like rosary in hard times. *What We Take With Us* tells of a journey from Double Creek, Kentucky, to a teaching life tending "wildflowers not in the meadows, but sidewalk cracks." Full of humor and sadness, sweetness and bitterness, the poems take us on a visual and sensory journey. Life with family, food and folkways wrap us in a quilt of memory.

— JANE HICKS
author of *Bone and Blood Remember* and *Driving with the Dead*

What We Take With Us

Sylvia Woods

EASTOVER
— PRESS —

Rochester, Massachusetts
www.eastoverpress.com

What We Take With Us

Copyright © 2021 by Sylvia Woods

POETRY

ISBN 978-1-958094-12-9

BOOK & COVER DESIGN: EK LARKEN
COVER IMAGE: FRANK WOODWARD

PUBLISHED IN THE UNITED STATES OF AMERICA BY

EASTOVER
— PRESS —

Rochester, Massachusetts
www.EastOverPress.com

for Elizabeth Adele Greene and Sadie Elyse Greene

CONTENTS

II

What We Take With Us

What We Take With Us

I make them memorize soliloquies,
some lines to keep, should they
be taken prisoner, like John McCain
in some foreign jail, no words to read,
no way to write, just the wild rantings
of Hamlet, Macbeth, to take
them through the darkest nights.
I urge them to know Dickinson,
Wordsworth, Whitman, some Keats,
seal the music in their souls.

High schoolers smirk at me. I smile,
for I know of prisons closer home
where they will need some words
that flash upon that inward eye in times
when solitude is no bliss, those times
of capture when we all are held
against our wills, in meetings so long
our eyeballs disengage,
in marriages bleak as dungeons,
in fears so dark we see no light,
the only comfort words we know for sure.

I

Mining

with apologies to Seamus Heaney

A kid spotted ink on my cheek.
"It's a sign of my work," I said, and swiped
careless green streaks.

I arrive home near dark, kick off heels
and mark papers into the night, tired eyes
squint and brows furrow by lamplight;
green ink dots like fly paper,
as I winnow poor words from pages.

Daddy got up before daylight,
put on work clothes pressed
in sharp creases, starched firm
as the knowing he was bound to mine seams
in Kentucky hills all the days of his life.

My father left work covered
in coal dust, face and hands black
as midnight—fine grit sparkled
near his wide smile, eyes dark as the mines.
At day's end he scrubbed grime
from knuckles where dust turned to oil,
blew black powder from his nose.
By the front door dark puddles
dripped from the soles of his boots.

I wear white collars to work,
come home with these marks,
my life bound to thick passages,
uncertain prose mined from essays
stacked thick as Kentucky hills.

Peeling

First she gouged out the eyes.
Then she skinned the spuds' peels
in one long spiral, the same way
she told tales that wound

round and round the family tree.
While sliced disks sizzled in hot lard,
she laid bare stories of distant kin
and sins as dark as cast iron.

One time Cousin Kit killed
a dog because it barked too much.
Another time he caught a skunk
and loosed him in a neighbor's barn.

That heathen bootlegged moonshine,
was too lazy to work mines or logwoods,
never darkened the church door.
Married two women the same month.

Still, he was our kin—his sins
a warning passed around for supper.

Prayer for the Hills

Hills protect us in this valley here.
The barn cat stares with emerald eyes,
steady as some distant planet in the sky.

Storms and blizzards send snow and hail.
Jim and Sue divorce, and Joe goes off to war.
Hills protect us in this valley here.

Farmers toil the earth and then lie,
sleeping long beneath the ridge,
steady as some distant planet in the sky.

The dog takes sick; we bury him.
Sister cries and brother wipes his eyes,
steady as some distant planet in the sky.

The neighbor's Chevy coughs and dies.
He trades it for a brand-new Ford.
The dealer sells the Chevy to a kid.

The house is silent now; children grown.
Our rooms echo like empty caves.
Hills protect us in this valley here.
Steady as some distant planet in the sky.

Morning

Gray dawn filters
through gauzy curtains,
flutters on the ceiling,
amorphous as moths.

From the kitchen come Mommy's feet
as she pads from stove to counter,
humming, *"I'm just going over Jordan.*
Just going...over home."

Outside, birds twitter in trees while I
snuggle in warm quilts, close to sister,
her breath a whisper.

Mommy's shoes swish as she sifts flour,
kneads biscuits. The coffee pot perks,
blur-blurb, fragrance wafting
like a morning kiss. Another sizzle,
sausage in the iron skillet.

While the house sleeps, she whispers,
"Frank," and bedsprings creak twice
as he rolls over once, turns, sighs hard,
slams both feet on the floor.

Then a yawing stretch and the whoosh
of boots over socks, of sturdy tread
on wood and linoleum to steaming food

where the scrape of chair precedes
clatter of fork on plate, slam of screen door
leaving true silence in his wake.

Crumbs

She wore her face
expressionless
like a fortress
against the world.
She never wasted
a thing in her life,
not even crumbs
from the pineapple
upside down cake,
the only cake
she ever made.
She'd clean off
the table, dusting
the crumbs
into the cat's dish.

Weeds and Wildflowers

Dandelions polkadot my lawn
in spring, announce it's time to mow.
They stretch their necks
through cracks in concrete,
spread their seeds in the wind,
intent on growing and living.

My class is filled with dandelions,
kids who grow up without fancy
fertilizers like ballet lessons
and new basketball shoes.
I watch their faces flower
through the cracks. I see them
keep on. Even when mowers
blade them to the ground,
they rise up again and again.

Irony of Beliefs

I don't believe in witchcraft, but laud the power of faith.
I don't believe in miracles, but accept that telephones
so tiny they fit in palms can send my image
across ten thousand miles in seconds.
I don't believe in little green men and Martians, yet
accept with a straight face your talk about gigabytes,
disks that hold a novel in the space of a key.

Forbidden

We were sneaky children,
going against our parents'
warnings, testing fate.

One time we stole dried apples.
We clever thieves slipped
across our mother's waxed tiles
into the cool darkness of
the still kitchen.
We grabbed the very thing
that we knew could swell,
stop up our insides,
kill us dead.
Stuffing pockets,
then mouths, nothing
could keep us from the forbidden
shriveled disks.

I wonder how we stayed alive.

And how, when we heaved our bodies clinging
to fragile ropes of forest vines, we fell
like tree limbs onto boulders. Trying
to doom ourselves, we yet rose
invincible. By evening
we had threatened our lives a dozen times.

I don't see how, except by the grace
of God you didn't break your neck
in those dives from the tree top,
soaring over Red Bird River.
I held my breath each time I saw the arc,

the limb that bore your weight, heard the snap
and waited for your face to emerge
from the depths of Will's Hole, a pool
so deep no one had ever touched its floor.

A Teacher's Monday Prayer

Dear God, I gotta ask where did the weekend go,
those golden days that beckoned like a beach
vacation? Where, Lord, went sleeping late?
This I ask in all humility, seeking to know
the truth, for that's the way I want to live.

On Saturday, I fell to my knees, took a soapy sponge
to dried jelly in front of the fridge. I folded baskets
of towels and jeans fresh from the dryer. I went out
among the multitudes, fought Kroger's crowded
parking lot to gather loaves of bread and fish—
enough to feed my family for the week.

I'd barely closed my eyes when the Sabbath sun
shone into my window, forced me to rise.
Papers consumed my day of rest, papers stacked
in piles around my chair, the church of English
teachers. Forgive me, instead of hymns, I meditated
to soothe my tormented soul, frantic to find
a single thesis statement.

Lord, as I walk and teach in this valley, I pray
please help me help all children to use spellcheck,
even those defiant ones who cannot spell *definitely*.

I accept it is your will that my weekend slipped away
when I was unaware. Will you at least bless me,
grant me the sustenance to find my car keys?

Periwinkle

You give life to pink, nostalgia
to purple, sass to blue. You clear
the haze from gray. You, the color
of freshest spring, dot the bank
like French impressionists, cover
the ground so well no one can mow
your blooms.

A-4

I dance with Daddy
in that old café on 421.
His fingers select A-4,
and dizzy spin of vinyl,
Hank's *"Hey Good Looking,"*
reverberates on painted cinderblock.

He orders four hotdogs, with,
then lip-synching Hank,
"How's about cookin'
something up with me,"
extends his hand, reels
me around the room.
I careen in smoky circles.

Checkered tiles echo
a blur of wingtips.
His shirt starched white,
ebony hair curls
over one eye,
like Elvis.

"Feel the rhythm,"
he urges. At forty
his feet twirl faster, lighter
than mine at thirteen.
Smells pulse like gut strings
ringing through a doghouse bass,
chili, onions frying,
bootleg bourbon and Juicy Fruit,
Old Spice and Irish Spring.
Red lights blink
in the neon sign.

Thesaurus

The bookish boy
in second period
mines the rich veins
of his Roget's and writes
without irony,
"Earnest
has the proclivity
to versify his sagas
in curtailed sentences
and plain discourse."

Dreams

In the deep mist
between two
and five a.m.
her spirit floats,
a spongy cloud
on a spring day.
Featherlight, we
drift—lucid dream
spirits embrace.

A wraith in white
on a dais,
she's encircled
by fair visions
in gilded turbans,
singing hymns.
From bejeweled
fingers, she slips
into my palm
a ruby ring
a rich blessing
and disappears
before daylight.

Too real, these night
scenes' yellow light,
like butter swirls
in molasses,
sweet tea in July.

Grammar Girdle

Shedding my grammar girdle, hill talk sighs
onto blue lines, fat on the page, word endin's gone,
the very words poured out in uncles' and aunts' stories
on porches and at dinner tables on Double Creek.

Looking the lines like Mama looked soup beans,
I throw out the little rocks and pieces of twigs,
run my fingers over the mess,
and feel the perfect shapes, silky, smooth.

Them prepositions, sister, are the hardest to rout.
Like dandelions, they turn up in batches,
pop onto the page and take up lease
as if they have a quit-claim deed.

I pull in my gut, wince at what I up and done;
my pen a willow switch, I whip
across lines, scratch away the lazy words,
and scream like my Aunt Alice yelled at the cat
that climbed to the top of the Frigidaire,
"Get down off from up on top of there!"

Laundry Day

The wringer washer rumbled
before breakfast finished. My brothers
carried buckets from the well.
My mother's tiny hands were red
and raw from winter's cold.
She scrubbed grease stains
from Daddy's work clothes, dipped
them in Faultless, added bluing
to the sulfur water to turn towels
and sheets white as snow. She
sent sheets through the wringer,
stretched the corners tight on the line
that wound a quarter mile up the hill.
Sheets and jeans waved like sails
in a seaside harbor, assuring when
bedtime came our house would smell
of bleach and sun and a mountain breeze.
She bleached and starched Daddy's
shirts—on the line, they arched.
When the denim coveralls dried
she ironed them stiff enough to stand alone.
She always tisked and shook her head
when we passed a neighbor's house
where once-white sheets flapped
their gray disgrace.

Word Path

I marvel at the cadence of your speech,
dance of predicate and nouns
you picked to name things of your world,
and nod to the rhythm of your head
tap dancing as you talk.

I love the way your eyes light
as you tell stories. Your shoulders
mark metaphors
as they pour from your mouth,
the history of your people in your tongue.

I lean in to hear your sounds,
see the way your mouth moves,
the softened d's and t's, diphthongs,
hear how you breathe from word to word,
l's and r's roll through your throat like a hymn.

I pay attention to syntax. The path
in which you place your words
lays claim to the place you were born.

On the Tenth Anniversary of James Still's Passing
at the Outdoor Chapel at Hindman Settlement School

This last day of April
we gather to celebrate and remember.
Cutworms free fall;
we laugh, slap them away,
fat green bodies that wiggle
and slide their silky curves
on our warm backs.

How they cling, hang
all their hundred legs
in this holy shrine
where we have sung and swarped
in summers, where ballads
of lost love and old time
religion brought sweet
communion, where we wove words
like filaments on dewy spider webs
suspended over Troublesome Creek.

Were he present,
and who's to say he is not,
I reckon the old man
would chuckle at plentiful larvae
of these night flying moths. Mayhap
he would say
who he wants with him in heaven,
recite verses about butterflies on Wolfpen

and minnows that leap
in shallow pools, happy as we to be
in these hills and of these hills,
still.

Drowning

That winter Cove Lake iced over.
Snow piled high;
schools closed for weeks.
While the children played,
she brooded, cooked soup.

Her future gray as the sunless sky,
she stared into darkness 'til first light
when she rose to stoke the fire. At last
when sun glittered snow, she bundled
both girls in coats and woolen hats.

They meant to walk away the gray.

Beside the lake as sun cast spiky
shadows on the icy path, a squeal
ripped the air. Beneath the bridge,
the dark figure of a dog,
submerged but for his snout.

Frozen, she watched his fight.

He climbed half way, slipped,
broke more ice—disappeared,
a dark hole where he'd been.
Still he fought, desperate,
paws seeking ice. More screams.

Taking each child by the hand
she turned, her eyes squinting
toward the light.

To Those Who Missed the Meeting

The meeting was toast. Desiccated. Dry.
We measured the dimensions of the room
once more: eight hundred and twenty-five
square feet if you count the closets. We do.
We debated the merits of whiteboard vs. chalk.
Considered stains, dust. The new girl declares
she just can't write. No agreement beyond
the ones we have now are too short for Jason,
for Carol too tall. I floated into another
dimension as talk digressed to closet dreams,
storage doors that slide on tracks, hide messes,
new blinds that open and close by remote control.
And oh, we were elated to learn the air
in our future would be sucked from the depths
of earth's core—geothermal warmth. A debate
followed on the number of drawers one needs
to file worksheets and tests; we probably won't
get to choose, but we agreed Bebe needs more.
Dry. Dry. Dry. Alan had run off somewhere
far away. Wanda was a no show. So was her wit.
Beth sat behind me, so impossible to see
her subtle isometric facial ballet, the way
her eyebrows would raise in dismay, or smirk
in distrust and rage. I tried to snooze, to take
my mind into another dimension. Carol—
who stood the entire meeting, so never tapped
her toes, though she did cross her arms a few times
and her ankles once, I'm sure—reminded me
I won't be here in ten years. Despite that promise,
I respectfully declined the request for volunteers
to attend the fun at tomorrow's assembly.

Poetic Drift

Homer lived just up the creek
when we were in sixth grade.
Raised by his granny,
he wore clothes bought to last,
sturdy flannel and cheap Sears jeans.
A homely boy, his head
a ball of twine with ears,
a rusty speckled face,
the rest all legs and arms,
he blushed when the teacher called his name.

Homer loved a joke. Certain
words tickled him:
scanty, perpendicular.
Homer giggled. Our eyes
widened and we laughed with him,
for he crowed a raucous, contagious cackle.
The only one who never minded
when Mrs. Sparks made us memorize
verses by Frost and St. Vincent Millay,
eyes like stars a million miles away,
he twirled the toe of his brogans
on the oiled floor when he forgot a line,
chin pointed to the ceiling.
Homer *became* the poet,
heroic, sad,
til tears
shimmered on his cheeks.

In my crowded city class
a boy poet stumbles through his ode.
Tangled memory rises,

blackberry and honeysuckle twined.
Drafted to undeclared war,
Homer sailed the wine dark seas,
and came home in a steel casket
lowered in a hillside
to rest near his granddaddy.

Now the creek bed sings
the sad gurgle of water over ancient rocks
and drowns birdsong at dawn.

Untimely

Why do you suppose, darkness and dog barks
aside, that I get an idea right thick in the middle
of the time to leave my house? When I should
be getting ready to toss on clothes and go to work,
words so powerful and so strong pop up
and jam the shredding machine of my mind.
Why can't I put those words away, Saran Wrapped
airtight for later? If I unwrapped it, heard the little
swoop of air released, perhaps in the evening
when I had time, would the savored succulence
smell and taste as sweet? Or would the seal
have broken, the flavor all gone flat?

Beulah

She sits in a straight chair
romance book open,
coffee cold with rainbows,
alone most of the time
with oxygen tank's tubes and masks,
baskets of prescription pill bottles.

With company she is in her element,
cooking, walking as far as her tether
can reach. She gives the lot of us advice
on winning in business, in love.
She can tell you the best way to handle a divorce,
get a baby to sleep, or school an ex in a settlement.

"You know what your problem is…"

Her voice rasps years of cigarette smoke,
a husky note in every sentence. We winced,
but now we miss her advice, her wisdom
as she cataloged where each of us went wrong,
a litany of our "problems" handed out like dinner rolls.

Irony

Two fourteen-year-olds
address each other as *Man*.
At fifty, *boy*.

Take the Slow Road

Give yourself permission to take the long way
home, the slow road instead of the highway
where people rush and stress, where trucks
and cars compete. Do it. Take two-lane roads
away from the frenzy of the interstate,
from big-box stores and shopping centers.
Let your eyes trace the curves in the road,
lay a second glance on hay bales in wide fields.
Enjoy those long stretches where there's not
one car to pass. Imagine you know the first names
of guys washing their cars on a warm weekend
or people porch-sitting in metal lawn chairs
like ones you used to see. Stop at a small grocery
with a single gas pump and rusty signs. Stretch
your legs. Eavesdrop on the men propped outside
on benches. Browse the local produce—
nothing exotic here like kiwi, but all the turnips
and half-runners you can eat.

When You Are Alone

Listen to the wind howl.
Imagine a giant scream in anguish
over a long-lost love.
Plan a pity party just for him.
Invite yourself and all your past selves too.
Play a sad love song or a bluegrass gospel tune
loud with tambourines,
rocking guitars, banjoes crying
for loved ones gathered at the river
while you are here, on the other side,
your pain so large
it is the giant crying in the wind.

Young Teacher Quits

She said the words we long to say daily.
She spoke up, found her voice
while she still had it, said, "I quit."

She would not squander youth, waste
her time hunched over inky hieroglyphics,
decipher paragraphs foggy as November rain.

She won't go the way we did, our journey
hastened by sleepless nights spent worrying
on the young for whom our fears are pennies,
copper spinning on train tracks, red sparks
glowing in darkness as they disappear in the night.

Photo of My Father

He stands in easy slouch, hat at a cocky angle,
leather jacket lined in sheepskin, shirt collars
pressed by my mother's hands.

There he stands younger than I am now,
before he was sick, before he was depressed,
when he thought life was one big laugh.

He wore khaki pants, a brown belt, dress shoes—
it must have been Saturday—
he never wore work shoes anywhere but work.

Behind him, mountains, a balmy November day,
sky azure blue when no worries clouded
his eyes—before the thought of suicide.

Things I Learned the Hard Way

Food makes meetings go smoother,
gives arguers and complainers
a reason to close their mouths.
A sharp tongue wrapped
around bagels and cream cheese
loses its point.

At a meeting with four women
all bent on winning, I volunteer
to record minutes. History becomes
what's reported by we who write it.

II

Middle-aged Date

We went for a Sunday drive, the two
of us, out toward the dam at Norris,
a greening road of hills and curves.
His car was a convertible, of course;
the wind whipped my hair in strings
across my face, showed the bare spot
on his crown. I wore fancy clothes,
my eyes made up nice. He dressed
in a navy coat, blue cotton shirt pressed
crisp. Khakis too. When the cattle truck
passed over the centerline, he swerved
fast on a patch of hot oil, lost control.
Together, we slid in a muddy culvert—
my hair and his fancy car a mess—
with no way out but to climb over the side.

Stud Finder

You can buy a gadget to locate
the hollow between studs in the wall.
I wish I'd had something like that
back before I took up with Bill.

To put a shelf in the laundry room
the fool pounded nails for hours—
drywall transformed to spaghetti strainer.

When he was gone I marveled why
I hadn't the good sense to know
what was solid and what was hollow.

Children

They start to leave you little by little.
First, on chubby hands and knees,
crawling on rug and wood; then they
wobble and weave toward open doors,
big yellow buses and playgrounds
where you will be just an echo,
an echo that feeds them words
of love and Jello pudding.
Their memories wobble, and you
capture every thing you can, every scrap.

No Filter

I remember an early fall
and curvy roads on Highway 25.
I remember mist and fading trees,
a crumbling barn, a slanted house
against the mountainside.
I took pictures out the window,
lens filtered for fog.
I remember a sudden storm—
torrents, and gusts juddered
the Datsun side to side.
My windshield blurred
green and yellow like a Matisse.
Tires skidded on wet pavement.
To stop the wild tailspin,
I gripped the wheel, told myself
to steer in the direction of the skid.
I remember trembling like a fawn.
When at last the vehicle stopped,
headlights faced the wrong direction.
Eyes trained to yellow lines,
I drove home through the deluge.
I remember I hugged my child
to my pounding chest.
He was watching *Batman*,
legs crossed like sticks.
He barely looked up,
oblivious to my shifted view.

Socks in the Room of a Twelve-Year-Old: The Singles Scene

They crowd into the dim space
like a film noir scene.
Drab ones lounge on stools.
Others huddle in groups
near the heat. Squeezed in knots
of threes and fives in the corner,
the pseudo-intellectuals attempt
to brazen out their aloneness.
Vibrating to rock and roll,
some sprawl on the floor by the stereo.
One dangles from the ceiling fan.
A couple mate on the sofa.

Words, Words, Words
for Kay Moss, Wanda Grooms and Miriam Wankerl

There are words invented
for women like you.
You've been called
most of them, epithets
once banned by the FCC,
five letters hurled
like scud missiles by retreating
twerps too young to vote,
furtive words in blue-lined notes,
scrawled on painted stalls,
carved on desks, by critics
short on vocabulary and wit.

But there are far better words for you,
words that fail yet to capture
your grace, power, elegance, impact.
Saints, you reared the children of the Ridge,
and your own—in your spare time.
Multi-taskers, you could grade papers, plan
lessons, cook dinner, oversee homework,
and dream dreams, simultaneously.

Clever women, you discovered new ways
to breathe life in Emerson and Thoreau,
found the razzle-dazzle in Shakespeare,
the luminous in Faulkner, and even
a lambent flame in Hardy's prose.

Inheritance

I sink into Faulkner's cadence, embrace
his way of letting words roll in waves,
phrases rock like chairs at country stores.
Who will tell of my people, people of the hills
whose church hymns and superstitions entwine
inseparable, myth and religion, old and new?
It's up to the living to pass on the stories.
The Super Walmart up the street just took out
the country store, ripped it off its foundation
and with the porch, old guys on the coke cases
and straight chairs, old men who told
old tales and deconstructed new ones.

Haiku Adolescence

Adults wonder, moan—
teenagers never think past
this moment, this flash.

We urge, "Think ahead.
Think of your future." Say, "Kids,
NOW is not all that."

But what if, *what if*
we told them to drink deeply
of here, NOW. "Sip it."

What if? But what if
instead of planning what's next
we told our children,

"Savor today's taste,
sample the bittersweet tang
of adolescence...

Roll it on your tongue,
taste its nectar, the fleeting
syrup melting soon."

Worry Doesn't Spend at the Store

If it did, I would be a gazillionaire.
There are stacks in the basement.
The attic's full, dusty boxes left
from the last Gulf War when the first
Bush was in office. In the pantry,
I've got it in cans and powder,
saved from my children's early twenties
and their timed-release screw-ups.
The fresh stuff, earned from bad
decisions and late fees, I keep out
on the counter or in the fridge cooling.
My basement walls are scaled with black mold,
the way interest compounds. A vault of richness.

Cast Iron Mason-Dixon Line

My son, discussing kitchen needs
for his approaching marriage,
said, "Missy's mother
doesn't have a black skillet."

"Lord have mercy," I said.
"How in the world
does she make cornbread?"

"She doesn't," he sighed.
"She bakes muffins in a pan.
She doesn't need a black skillet."

When a poor boy from the South
thinks of home and the future,
he thinks of soup beans and cornbread.
I don't mind telling you
I worry about mixed marriages.

Upturned Button Box

Splayed in a kaleidoscope of shapes,
buttons fascinate the child. She swirls
the flat and filigreed designs and drapes
her fingers through and through, her tiny world's
delightful sensations, glassy, smooth or rough.
She shifts the colors, commences to divide, arrange
the blues, the purples, pinks and whites—enough;
order advances with each artful change.
The mother eyes the scene, the play a view
of human endeavor, the way we act. Chaos
scares us, so we catalog. This thing we do
separates people and things by size, by class,
by color, as though by making piles this way
we organize, laying straight a world in disarray.

Taking Yeats to Bed

I'm taking Yeats to bed tonight.
Last night it was Wordsworth,
the night before, a whole group
of men from the south. I'm flexible

but selective. I won't take to bed
with me, for example, anyone
ultraconservative or who insists
on extreme regularity. I like guys

who know something about music,
croon some blues in the middle
of the night, tap out syncopated jazz,
maybe even hum an old gospel tune.

I don't have to go out looking
these days; I've known most of
these guys for years. Still, a new guy
willing to risk it all can be thrilling.

I've got my standards, I draw the line
at a man who disrespects the South,
denigrates Appalachians, makes fun
of hicks and country bumpkins, poor
white trash or any of my friends.

I once threw a man out of bed when he
was in the middle of telling me his life
story. Yeah, it was pitiful, the life
he'd led, but he was boring. Sorry, Jack.

When a man goes to bed with me,
he better have something to say. He better
say it with style because I'm not afraid
to slam his book shut and go to sleep.

Knowing

A child of depression, her blue veined hands
map a life drawn from hilly acres. Age detailed hands
suckered tobacco, weeded corn, dug potatoes, endured
loss of child and man. Palms open to help neighbors, kin.

On her front porch, she leans forward in painted chair,
breaks the tip of a half-runner, tugs string
down its spine. The pile grows like green spaghetti.

"Did you know the Chinese stir fry green beans?"
asks a niece, the one who went to Europe junior year.
"And the French cut them slantwise with a knife,
call it *julienne*."

"I simmer beans with a little fat back,
cook them hours, steam up the windows,
bake cornbread hot and crusty in the skillet
Mama left me." Mae says, "That is what I know."

Reincarnation

I wonder, Mama, are you here on earth
reincarnated? New Age gurus say your spirit
might reside in that rangy tabby cat
the neighbor forgets to feed. Her cries cut through
my door. She limps inside, half starved.
I give her a can of tuna. Your green eyes stare
a measuring moment before she starts to eat.
Or did you come back in human form?
Could you be that pimply pizza delivery kid
who stammers, tongue-tied on the porch?
I hand him a ten, double my usual tip, just in case.

Birthdays in Three Voices
after Alicia Suskin Ostriker

Birthdays, said the artist,
are just a number for men
who date online
but won't look at a woman
older than forty. God knows
my birthday. Who else cares
how many times I've painted
the sun rising over ridgetops,
the decades I've taken brush
to pallet to record sycamores
dropping their leaves
over the riverbank.

Birthdays, said the iron
skillet, call for cake
and two even bakings
in the oven. Sugar,
sticky and sweet,
reminds even old people
that most things don't last
as long as a properly
seasoned skillet.

Birthdays, ha! A chance
to swoop crumbs
from the back door
stoop, swept there
by an old woman, her hair
waving in the wind, stiff
as the straw in the barn loft.

Birthdays, the crow proclaims,
are just another day
foraging for leftovers.

Romance: Old Lovers and Bad Verse

The past's a spent flame, a place
too far away to reach from here,

like this yellowed poem, relic
of a long-forgotten swain.

Not much to tell: midnight
beneath shadowy trees,

a kiss or two, our hands entwined,
ardent promises, cabernet

and candlelight. *Romance*—
a word woven in weekend moonlight

that evaporates like dew on the meadow
when exposed to sunshine.

Cleaning Day

What if I hire a strong man
or an energetic girl to edit my life,
correct the mistakes in judgment,
issue new report cards, revise the diaries
and write sincere apologies,
use linen paper and scented envelopes?

I'll mow the yard and wash the windows
if I can just get someone *else* to peer
into the dirty panes of my youth, wipe clean
the smudges on my storied past, the "should'ves"
and "if I had'ves" erased forever.

And while she's at it, take out the trash
I associated with in short-sighted moments of bliss.

I will scrub the floors myself, put a spit shine
on them if I can just hire a disinterested girl
or guy who knows how to wipe away grime
built up through the years like wax,
someone to put a shine on past excess.

So Manly He Stands to Pee

I drive past a dancing boy—six or seven—
on the sidewalk in front of Goody's,
see him turn, bend his elbows, arch his back,
and begin his business. Turning the corner,
I glance in the rearview mirror in time to spy
a perfect, golden arc stream onto the sidewalk.

I'm not shocked to see a boy's freedom
to relieve himself. Yet I'm certain a girl
any age would never feel that perfect ease.

Empty Nest Secret

From couch to kitchen bin, I toss the apple core,
miss it once and try again, breaking every rule
I taught the two of them. Hurray! Two points!
My bedclothes wander to the floor to drift
among the socks galore. Jerry Springer's
on TV all night. I eat frozen pizza and sugar-
frosted cereal, do all the things I denied the kids
because I wanted to teach responsibility.

But don't you worry, or miss a beat,
I'll redd up the house spic and span
before they come for a Sunday meal,
pick up socks and right the fan, serve
the only food I plan to cook all week.

Delcie's February Offering

I search the pantry shelves
for dried apples, hid in the dark,
desiccated as granny's cheeks.

Add golden molasses, butter from
the churn, brown eggs from my best hen.

Serve it on that old plate
Aunt Sudie give me on my wedding day,
me little more than a girl child.

Offer it to my old man,
brown hair white now, cheeks sunk
that used to be plump as Red Romes.

It ain't much, but it fills a taste
I got for a little July heat.

Addie at Two
after Donald Justice

And on the floor across the hardened wood
the child of two would roll her dolly back
and forth, in circles round, as if she could
circle earth in her traversing there and there,

and nights would find her snuggled in the bed,
and we would read of dogs and cats in hats
that break the rules. She slept with dreams
of words that rhyme, wheels that go round and back.

What I Will Do to Worry

I will wrap it in tissue so well
sharp points will not protrude;
I'll find some batting, cottony thick,
wrap it around and around in layers,
swaddle it like a mummy, leave
the whole thing in a wooden box.

A soft thud when it lands reassures me.
It will wait awhile, then wriggle,
squirm free of its box, and the next thing
I know I will have it in my bed again,
feel it move over me,
its jagged edges pit my skin.

Shall I set it on the mantle for all to see,
admire how its diamond points drew my blood?

Redbud Winter

with apologies to Louise Gluck

This is the moment we see again
the redbud's purple flowers
reaching for azure sky,
return of dogwood blooms.

It saddens me no end
how soon they are gone—
how quickly spring brights,
withers and disappears.

Urbane Appalachian

He drinks his coffee from a Starbucks mug,
wears designer duds with suave aplomb,
trots out tolerance like a pedigreed pup.
With a wave of one soft hand, he avers
his deep *respect* for folks of all cultures.
He's not *prejudiced*, would *never* use ethnic slurs.
On the other hand, this fellow thinks it clever
to make incest jokes, spurns people
earning a hard living in a hard land,
refers to callused and sunburned men as "rednecks."
"Hillbilly bashing," he says. "No offense meant,"
the smirk on his face smooth as his palms,
a little sport for an elitist at ease
with his alphabet degrees and city ways.

Compost

Thoughts of you roil
in my mind like potato
peels and carrot tops mixed
with coffee grounds—
aromatic, earthy smells.
Last week's kitchen garbage.
Its pungent odor lingers, rots.

Resumé

Her first job: feeder of babies,
full-time wiper of bottoms and faces.
A promotion: chauffeur to ballet
dancers and boy scouts, available
all hours for church camp
and band trips out of state,
always back by dawn.
After sixteen years, she advanced
to bank teller and pay master,
paying and paying by degrees.
Semi-retired, she curates a childhood
museum where she watches over Luke
Skywalker, Barbie, and all her mansions.
Then she begins again: part-time wiper
of faces and bottoms. Storyteller.

Taking or Leaving?

If you were going to leave the teacher's life,
the paper stacks, email demands, the teens
with acne and angst like boiled-over syrup,
what would you take with you? Which
of the scribbled essays, pockmarked with red?
Or some dogeared anthology? Maybe instruction
sheets on what to do the day the fire alarm is real,
the day the lockdown lasts until after the last bell?
Would you, perhaps, take a small journal that tells
how to teach similes and metaphors in easy stages.
Or would you just set down your grading pen
and walk? I'm telling you, you are leaving every day
a part of yourself as permanent as indelible ink.
Ghost lessons you didn't know you taught.

Without You (u) I Choose Sin

In my new life I raise Cain, dance
a blizzard, shimmy hips in digs
where jazz riffs rise to the rafters
in syncopated beats—old time
fiddle ditties and string bass—
all I need in this reveler's paradise.
Bright ideas ignite
like matches on my brain case,
tell me to dance, boogie down,
swig vodka, croon at the moon,
giggle, stay awake all night,
play cards, shoot pool, tell lies,
drink life fast, like cheap wine.

ABOUT THE AUTHOR

SYLVIA WOODS taught high school English in East Tennessee for forty-three years. She is a native of Eastern Kentucky where her people have lived for over two hundred years. Her poems have appeared in many literary journals and anthologies. This is her first full-length collection. In her spare time Woods enjoys occasional volunteer teaching, hiking and spending time with her brilliant granddaughters.

ACKNOWLEDGMENTS

Thank you to the following journals and anthologies for first publishing versions of these poems:

Alalit.com: Changes; Prayer for the Hills, a Villanelle

Appalachian Heritage: On the Tenth Anniversary of James Still's Passing; [Wearing My] Grammar Girdle

Appalachian Journal: Beulah

Black Moon Magazine: Birthdays in Three Voices

Calliope: Forbidden

Centrifugal Eye: Stud Finder

Cutleaf: Taking Yeats to Bed; To Those Who Missed the Meeting; Young Teacher Quits; Without You (u) I Choose Sin

Lincoln Memorial University's Poem A Day: Drowning

Low Explosions: Writings on the Body: Morning

Motif v1: Writing by Ear, An Anthology of Writings About Music: A-4

Motif v2: Come What May, An Anthology of Writings About Chance: Poetic Drift

Now & Then: Knowing

Off Channel: What We Take With Us

Still: The Journal: Mining; No Filter; Word Path

Tennessee English Journal: Thesaurus

THANKS

Without the help and encouragement of Denton Loving and Donna Crow, the Gap House Writers, I never would have completed this collection. I thank Denton for his patience and editing skills. I am grateful to EastOver Press for publishing this collection. I am grateful to all my writing teachers who taught me where to put words, especially Maurice Manning, Connie Green, George Ella Lyon, Jesse Graves and Darnell Arnoult. I am grateful to my writing friends Jane Hicks, Jane Sasser, Jason Howard, Silas House and the members of HOO who patiently listened and read my poor verse. I thank the board members of the Tennessee Mountain Writers who have offered constant encouragement for more than thirty years. Because of the rich storytelling tradition of my parents, my uncles, aunts and cousins, I was lucky to grow up knowing my history and the people I never met who live in my memory. I'm also thankful to my siblings: Hoye, Beulah, Roy, Lottie and Stanley, who always loved me even though they think I'm weird. And thanks to my posse who toiled with me at ORHS and inspired me to be a better teacher: Carol, Ann, Miriam, Jane, Beth, Alice and Vondle. And, finally, to the thousands of students who passed through my classrooms, you will always be in my thoughts.